How to Survive Grey Divorce

What You Need to Know About Divorce After 50

by
Marlo Van Oorschot, J.D.

Book design by Glyphix

Cover art derived from *American Gothic*, 1930 by Grant Wood
All rights reserved Wood Graham Beneficiaries/Licensed by
VAGA, New York, NY

Edited by John Toth

Nothing contained in this book is to be considered as the rendering of legal advice, either generally or in connection with any specific issue or case. Readers are responsible for obtaining advice from their own lawyers or other professionals. This book is intended for educational and informational purposes only.

Published by Law Offices of Marlo Van Oorschot, APLC
10513 Santa Monica Boulevard
Los Angeles, CA 90025
310-820-3414
mvo@mvolaw.com
www.mvolaw.com

Copyright © 2012 by Marlo Van Oorschot.
All rights reserved. No part of this book may be reproduced, stored in a retrieval system or transmitted in any form or by any means, electronic, mechanical, photocopying, recording or otherwise, without written permission from the publisher.

ISBN 978-0-9849777-0-3
Library of Congress Control Number: 2012904255
Printed in the United States of America

TABLE OF CONTENTS

FOREWORD vii

ACKNOWLEDGEMENTS xi

The Phenomenon: What Is Grey Divorce? 1

    The Definition 3

    Grey Divorce is Increasing 4

    Unique Issues in Grey Divorce 5

Husband and Wife: Who Are Breadwinning and Non-Breadwinning Spouses? 7

    The Definition 9

    Case Study 10

    The Challenges 11

Financial Support: How Is Support Determined? 13

    Support Distinctions 15

    Spousal Support Factors 17

    Long-Term Support 19

Social Security: How Are Benefits Divided? 21

- Not Subject to Division 23
- Derivative Benefits 24
- 10-Year Mark 26
- An Example 27

The House: Asset or Liability? 31

- Property Division 33
- In and Out Spouse 35
- Equal Division? 36
- Credit Score Impact 37
- Risks vs. Benefits 38

Insurance: Who Is Covered? 41

- Health Issues 43
- Coverage Concerns 43
- Breadwinner Health Care Costs 44
- Non-Breadwinner Health Care Costs 45

Taxes: Who Pays and Why? 47

- Child Support 49

Spousal Support 52

Property Division 54

Attorneys' Fees 55

Innocent Spouse Relief 56

Bankruptcy: What Is the Impact? 59

Bankruptcy Stay 62

Non-Dischargeable Debts 63

Estate Planning: Are Your Wishes Honored? 67

Grey Divorce Considerations 69

Real Property 70

Trusts & Wills 71

Trust Funding 72

Beneficiary Designations 73

Durable Powers of Attorney 74

Advance Health Care Directives 76

Your Choices 77

Advance Health Care Directive–Lets You: 78

Estate Planning After Divorce 80

Professional Advice: Who Can You Talk To? 83

Estate Planner 85

Insurance Agent..86

Financial Advisor 87

Accountant..87

Family Law Attorneys and Mediators.......................88

Final Thoughts 91

Glossary..95

About Marlo Van Oorschot, author of "How To Survive Grey Divorce" 107

FOREWORD

You probably never expected to need a book like this. We all know the statistics on divorce, but statistics are of little consolation when they apply to you. Divorce at any age is traumatic, but "grey" divorce–that is divorce after 50–can be even more difficult. While youth may be wasted on the young, they have time on their side. Some divorcees report a sense of financial panic–they've felt their emotional world turn upside down for months or even years, but often don't realize the financial impact until well into the divorce.

There are few ways you can prepare for the emotional tumult, but fortunately there are many things you can do if you are preparing for a divorce or have experienced a divorce to help you become financially secure and to create a sense of economic stability in an otherwise difficult time.

Marlo Van Oorschot has created a roadmap for you to follow to make sure you are doing everything you can to create a firm financial foundation. Your most pressing legal and financial questions are answered in clear, non-technical or jargon-filled language. Marlo has been in the trenches for years and has taken the best of what she knows and distilled it into a blueprint for your recovery and growth.

I've spent over 15 years helping individuals become financially independent in various stages of divorce. Through my firm Pacifica Wealth Advisors, some come to me well in advance while others wait until they've bounced a few checks. Regardless of when they seek help, they all want one thing: to feel financially stable without their partner. For some that means paying off debt and paying their bills. For others, it means taking advantage of their new "freedom" and going back to school, traveling the world, or joining a non-profit. Spend the time getting your finances reviewed and in order. The peace of mind knowing you are financially secure is a critical first step in creating a better life.

Helen Keller once said "When one door of happiness closes, another opens; but often we look so long at the closed door that we do not see the one which has been opened for us." May this book be just one door of opportunity you will notice and walk through.

–Robert Pagliarini
Best-Selling Author, The Six Day Financial Makeover & The Other 8 Hours: Maximize Your Free Time to Create New Wealth and Purpose

President of Pacifica Wealth Advisors (www.pacificawealth.com)

Financial Expert on Dr. Phil, Good Morning America, 20/20, *and* Dr. Drew's LifeChangers

ACKNOWLEDGEMENTS

When my business coach, Ed Poll, of LawBiz™, suggested I write this book, I thought it was a wonderful idea because I had produced a lot of written material about Grey Divorce. Then I thought, "How will I do this while managing a busy family law practice?" But the issue is so important I decided to make the time–and here is the end result.

There are so many people in my life whom I thank for your support, but most important is my husband. My husband has been by my side through this entire journey for which I am eternally grateful. My husband and I work in the same office and he lends his talents to my law firm while still operating his own company. My husband is a partner–in the truest sense of the word. Marriage is truly a partnership which takes work and hopefully rewards others, as it has me. Unfortunately, as this book examines, this is not always the case.

I want to thank my colleagues, too many to name, who have taken the time out of their busy professional lives to read the chapters in this book which relate to their own professions to insure the information contained in this book is accurate and relevant to the topic.

Thank you to everyone involved in making this book come to life–I hope you each know who you are.

Lastly, to Ed Poll, who inspired this project and guided me to the end–Thank you.

1

The Phenomenon: What Is Grey Divorce?

"A man's life, like a piece of tapestry, is made up of many strands which interwoven make a pattern; to separate a single one and look at it alone, not only destroys the whole, but gives the strand itself a false value."

–Justice Learned Hand
Proceedings in Memory of Mr. Justice Brandeis, 317 U.S. xi (1942)

The Definition

Grey divorce[1] is a term referring to the demographic trend of an increasing divorce rate for older ("grey-haired") couples who have been married often for many years. A very public example of this was Tipper and Al Gore's 2010 decision to divorce after 40 years of marriage. Although the reason for this phenomenon is disputed, there is no doubt this is occurring not only here in the United States but also in other countries. Observers in Japan have deemed it "Retired Husband Syndrome," brought on when husbands retire and are home with their wives all day for the first time in years, leading one or both spouses to feel like they are living with a virtual stranger. It is the stress of the change in lifestyle, which is one of the cited reasons for an increasing divorce rate among people over age 50.

---

[1] Words or phrases used in this book, identified in ***bold italic*** print, are identified in the glossary at the end of this book. For ease of the reader, only the first reference to the word or phrase will be in the bold italic font.

Grey Divorce is Increasing

Statistics from the National Center for Family & Demographic Research demonstrate the increasing prevalence of grey divorce in the United States. According to the Center's research, the divorce rate among persons ages 50 and older has more than doubled between 1990 and 2008. For every 1,000 married persons age 50 and older, nearly 10 experienced divorce in 2008. Whereas fewer than 1 in 10 persons who divorced in 1990 were age 50 or older, more than 1 in 4 persons who divorced in 2008 were age 50 or older–a total of some 600,000 people. Researchers at the Center, assuming the 2008 divorce rate for people age 50 and older remains unchanged, projected that in 2030, more than 800,000 people in this age group will experience divorce as the population ages. And with the rate of divorce actually increasing, the number of people over age 50 experiencing divorce two decades from now will likely be much greater.[2]

---

[2] Susan L. Brown and I-Fen Lin, "Divorce in Middle and Later Life: New Estimates from the 2009 American Community Survey," National Center for Family & Demographic Research (Bowling Green State University), http://www.bgsu.edu/downloads/cas/file94173.pdf

Unique Issues in Grey Divorce

Although grey divorces can be amicable, they raise major and unique concerns regarding retirement, support, workforce re-entry, dual household expenses, declining health and increasing healthcare costs. This book will analyze these issues in the context of how divorcing spouses over the age of 50 can recognize and minimize potential problems in order to maximize their quality of life following the divorce. To achieve this goal, cooperation between the spouses in a spirit of partnership that once made the marriage workable is required. The grey divorce is best looked at as a tapestry–the whole–rather than one strand at a time. Understanding the potential problems and assessing ways to resolve those problems offers the best chance to create that kind of cooperation necessary for a successful resolution of a grey divorce. The information in this book is intended to help make such an outcome possible. Discussion in this book will be straightforward and objective in tone, and will be generalized to cover the many different people who will be reading it. But because the issues are so personal, there are points that will be directly addressed to you, the reader–because it is for you that this book is written.

2

Husband and Wife: Who Are Breadwinning and Non-Breadwinning Spouses?

While the husband is still declared by statute to be the head of the family...he, like the King of England, is largely a figurehead.

–James K.J. Hines
in *Curtis v Ashworth, 165 Ga 782,787 (1928)*

The Definition

Often grey divorce involves a discussion about how a late-in-life divorce is either empowering for women or is devastating (psychologically, financially and sexually) for them. Deciding which assumption is correct involves analyzing to what extent the divorcing female spouse has earned her own income. Historically older women who divorce have not had the opportunity to earn any or substantial income through work outside the home. The male spouse in such a situation is considered to be the "***breadwinner***"–the spouse with the higher income. The female spouse is the "***non-breadwinner***." These distinctions assume much greater importance in divorce than they did during the marriage. *For purposes of this book, these historical roles will be used*, but clearly the roles of which spouse is the breadwinner and non-breadwinner are often reversed.

Case Study

Consider spouses who have been married for 30 years. The husband, age 65, has been the sole wage earner (the breadwinner) in the household while the wife, now age 60, has raised children who are now adults and supported the husband's career. Both have decided to divorce. A decade earlier they undertook to adopt a child who is now age 10 and is financially dependent on both parents. Both spouses had hoped to retire by this time in their lives; however, because of the divorce, retirement may need to be postponed and the financial resources of the parties will need to be stretched to support two separate households. The divorce will mean the loss of health insurance for the wife because she was dependent upon her husband's policy. Husband and wife have a home with a mortgage. Careful financial planning is needed to ensure the best possible decisions are made during the divorce. Bankruptcy would be disastrous. The advancing age of the couple requires review and changes to estate plans, insurance and life plans.

The Challenges

When divorcing, these breadwinning and non-breadwinning spouses face real world issues concerning retirement, the need to support their late-in-life child, job opportunities, the financial strain of two households, declining health and increasing health insurance and health expenses. Each has legitimate concerns about how to financially manage their affairs after the divorce. The non-breadwinner may never receive future assets or income other than the divorce award. A settlement that meets estimated current and future financial needs may not always be feasible, making it possible she will have to work. The breadwinner faces similar difficult choices at age 65 and may be unable financially to retire due to support obligations he may owe to his wife and minor child. Resolving such challenges is typically at the heart of a successful grey divorce.

3

Financial Support: How Is Support Determined?

Q: Under what circumstances could I get spousal support?

A: The court will decide if you need it and whether it is fair.

–The Alaska Court System Self-Help Center, Family Law

One of the critical issues in grey divorce is ***spousal support*** (often referred to as alimony). As compared to ***child support***, which is largely formulaic and intended to meet the needs of the minor child, spousal support is a much more complex determination intended to meet the financial needs of the non-breadwinner. In grey divorce, spousal support is a challenging issue because the reality often is that the non-breadwinner will likely need financial support for the rest of her life because her expenses will continue to increase (i.e., health care) and the likelihood of her becoming self-supporting is not great. These realities clash with the breadwinner's own advancing age, increased expenses and his ability to continue working.

Support Distinctions

Late-in-life divorce raises financial conflicts. The breadwinner must provide financial support to the non-breadwinner while either facing actual retirement (forced or voluntary) or planning aggressive retirement funding in the final (typically maximum income) working years. The non-breadwinner has these same concerns and may have to re-enter the workforce to assist in meeting increasing financial needs.

In California, child support is of primary importance in divorce, often taking priority over retirement or other financial plans. There are potentially several ways to meet this support obligation, but there is no doubt the choices are not easy and will differ from the plans the couple had been implementing prior to the divorce. The non-breadwinner and breadwinner may both need to reduce living expenses to match reduced income if or when the breadwinner retires; the breadwinner may need to delay retirement; or the non-breadwinner may need re-training or additional education to get a job and supplement the breadwinner's support. Facing these realities sooner rather than later is best.

Compared to child support, spousal support is not formulaic. It reflects many factors, including but not limited to, income, each spouse's expenses, each spouse's ***earning capacity***, the ***marital standard of living*** and history of saving (i.e. retirement funding). The non-breadwinner should document any history of savings as part of her need for retirement planning that she may want the breadwinner to continue funding. While there is no guarantee the breadwinner will be required to fund savings for the non-breadwinner, it is certainly a factor in determining support.

The unprepared non-breadwinner may be expected to make reasonable efforts toward supporting herself. If age and/or health preclude re-entering the workforce, the non-breadwinner may face a significantly reduced standard of living–especially if the breadwinner has retired or is physically unable to work. In grey divorce, the realities of life are often the dictating forces over which neither the parties nor the law has any control. This often results in very sad and unfortunate results in these late-in-life divorces.

Spousal Support Factors

The determination of spousal support is made up of many factors including the income of each spouse and the financial needs of each spouse measured by the marital standard of living the parties shared during the marriage. The court weighs this issue against if and when a spouse might be self-supporting, because the question of self sufficiency directly impacts the amount of spousal support and the length of time spousal support is paid. There are other factors which impact a decision about spousal support:

- **Age and Health** Advancing age and declining physical, emotional and mental health, often restricts the longevity of one's career or ability to earn. Age and health also impact the cost of health insurance and health care. These issues can cut both ways: either creating a need for support or the diminishing the ability to pay support.

- **Earning Capacity** Even if health issues do not interfere with a person's ability to work, there is a real question of the opportunity to work. Many companies are opting to hire younger employees with more sophisticated technological skills. The ability for an aging person to compete in today's workforce may be questionable and therefore impact the issue of spousal support–again in terms either of greater need for it or lesser resources to pay for it.

- **Lifestyle** For many years leading to their "golden years", people establish a certain lifestyle based on financial resources and expect it to continue. The recent recession significantly affected almost everyone's lifestyle and wealth, but baby boomers facing divorce do not have the same time to recover from the financial losses so many have experienced. They may be unable to make their reduced wealth meet the often increasing expenses of two homes and two lifestyles.

Long-Term Support

In California, there it is assumed that a marriage which lasts more than 10 years, is a ***long-term marriage*** requiring long-term spousal support. It is further assumed that a marriage which lasts less than 10 years is a ***short-term marriage*** and spousal support is payable for a time equal to one-half the length of the marriage. In any divorce these assumptions can be contested. As an illustration, a short-term marriage may be treated as a long-term marriage because as the non-breadwinner ages and her health, earning capacity and wealth decline, it is less likely she will ever be self-supporting. As a result, in a marriage that is technically a short-term marriage (less than 10 years), the court can view it as a marriage requiring ongoing support (akin to a long-term marriage). The key reason for this is the decreasing likelihood that the non-breadwinner will or can become self-supporting during the remainder of her lifetime. Therefore, grey divorce is a very difficult financial situation for both spouses because it presents complex financial issues that do not exist in other divorces brought on primarily by age and health issues. Creative problem solving with the assistance of legal and financial professionals may help reconcile the complexities of these cases, but it is unlikely they can be completely eliminated.

4

Social Security: How Are Benefits Divided?

Taxes are what we pay for civilized society, including the chance to insure.

–Oliver Wendell Holmes

Social Security benefits are a source of income intended to replace or supplement a person's income when they reach the age of eligibility. Social Security benefits should always be part of the discussion in grey divorce because the benefits are either being received at the time of the divorce, or will be soon received.

Not Subject to Division

In California, assets and debts acquired during the marriage are generally considered ***community property***, which means they are subject to an equal division by a family court when there is a divorce. ***Social Security benefits*** are an exception to this rule. Social Security benefits are derived from payroll taxes collected by the federal government (these taxes are recognizable on paycheck stubs as FICA, or "Federal Insurance Contributions Act") and are paid to eligible individuals based upon contributions that they, their spouses or their ex-spouses make into the Social Security system. Primary Social Security benefits belong to the working spouse (i.e., the spouse who paid into Social Security). They are not a community property asset, and will not be divided in a divorce. This means the working spouse/breadwinner will have the right to a Social Security benefit as a result of contributions to the Social Security System while working. Luckily, the Social Security system does not exclude the non-breadwinner, who did not work or earned less than the breadwinner, from receiving benefits, if certain criteria are satisfied.

Derivative Benefits

If prior to the divorce being final, the non-breadwinner who was married for 10 years or longer to a working/breadwinning spouse may be entitled to receive ***derivative Social Security benefits***. This benefit is based upon the working/breadwinning spouse's contributions into the Social Security system.[3] These derivative benefits do not affect the amount of benefits the working/breadwinning spouse receives. For the non-breadwinning spouse to be eligible, the basic requirements in addition to being divorced from the working/breadwinning spouse are:

---

[3] http://www.socialsecurity.gov/retire2/divspouse.htm

- The spouses must have been married for at least 10 years (therefore "former" spouses), measured from the date of marriage to the ***date marital status is terminated***;
- The working/breadwinning spouse is entitled to Social Security retirement or disability benefits;
- The non-breadwinner former spouse has filed an application for Social Security benefits;
- The non-breadwinning former spouse is 62 years old, or older;
- The non-breadwinning former spouse is unmarried at the time of applying for the derivative benefits;
- The non-breadwinning former spouse is not entitled to Social Security benefits, or is entitled to Social Security benefits based on their own social security benefit, which is less than one-half of the working/breadwinning spouse's social security benefit.

10-Year Mark

Being married for 10 years is the critical threshold to qualifying for derivative benefits. Many people do not realize this benefit exists yet the benefit is a very important part of assessing financial resources in grey divorce. As a result, if the marriage is nearing the 10-year mark, it is critical to be aware this benefit exists. Both the breadwinner and the non-breadwinner should want this benefit to be accessible by the non-breadwinner. The reason is because the non-breadwinner's right to this benefit does not reduce the breadwinner's benefit; and making sure the non-breadwinner qualifies for this benefit increases financial resources to the non-breadwinner which will help to reduce the breadwinner's spousal support obligation.

If the divorcing spouses' marriage is approaching the 10-year mark, a spouse may request that the court enter an order delaying the date on which marital status terminates so they can receive the derivative benefit. Some spouses want to terminate the marital status before all other issues are determined, which could jeopardize eligibility for the derivative benefits. However, family courts have authority under the law to impose any "just and equitable" condition on the request for an early termination of the marital status and may even delay the early termination date of marital status if there is good reason to do so. Ensuring that future Social Security benefits are received may be a good reason to ask a judge for permission to delay the termination of the marital status if the 10-year mark is approaching. Again, because the derivative benefit does not reduce the working spouse's Social Security benefit, it is a financial win-win to delay the termination of the marriage until the non-breadwinning former spouse can potentially access a stream of income in the future. Once the 10-year mark is met, it is advisable to review the Social Security Administration's current rules about these and other benefits (such as survivor benefits).

An Example

To help explain these complicated rules, let's follow the story of John, Lisa, Wendy and Henry. John and Lisa were married for 14 years. They are now getting divorced. John is entitled to receive $750 per month in Social Security benefits, based on his earnings. Lisa is entitled to receive $250 per month in Social Security benefits, based on her own earnings and contributions to the Social Security system.

Based on John's earnings, Lisa will be eligible to receive a derivative benefit of $375 a month, half of his benefit, if she is unmarried. John will get his full benefit. If John later marries Wendy, and they divorce after 10 years, Wendy would also be entitled to receive $375 per month based on John's earnings, half of his benefit. No matter how many women he marries, John still gets his $750 per month.

If Lisa (John's first wife) marries Henry and later divorces Henry after 10 years or longer, she can collect based on the earning histories of either John or Henry or her own account, whichever is higher.

If John dies after he and Lisa divorce, but before Lisa marries Henry, she will be entitled to widow's benefits (survivor benefits), which approximate his full Social

Security benefit if she is age 60 or older (age 50 if disabled). She'll continue getting those widow benefits even if she marries Henry, as long as she doesn't remarry before age 60 (age 50 if disabled). And Wendy, John's real widow, will also receive widow's benefits. If Lisa married Henry before the age of 60, she could not receive survivor benefits as a result of John's death, unless her later marriage to Henry ends by death, divorce or ***annulment***. Then, Lisa may collect benefits on John or Henry's record, whichever is higher.

5

The House:
Asset or Liability?

A man builds a fine house; and now he has a master, and a task for life; he is to furnish, watch, show it, and keep it in repair, the rest of his days."

–Ralph Waldo Emerson
Society and Solitude

The division of property is a major issue in grey divorce, and for most couples over the age of 50 their house is the largest asset they own. Traditionally, for the majority of homeowners, the value of their home is two-thirds of their total assets. And the latest figures from the Census Bureau show that 76% of people age 50 to 59 and 80% of those aged 60 to 69 are homeowners–with well over 80% of all homeowners being married couples. Such statistics show that, even in today's economic climate, the majority of couples in grey divorce are homeowners, and determining who gets the house is a major issue.[4]

Property Division

In the current economic climate of depressed real estate values, the breadwinner may find it a good idea to keep the real estate investments including the family residence (and

---

[4] National Association of Homebuilders, "Home Ownership: The Engine of Wealth Accumulation," (http://www.nahb.org/generic.aspx?genericContentID=60818&print=true); and U.S. Census Bureau, "Homeownership by Age," (http://www.census.gov/compendia/statab/2012/tables/12s0992.pdf)

the tax benefits) as part of the divorce settlement because the real estate is purchased in the divorce at the current fair market value and it is the breadwinner who is most likely able to afford keeping the property. However, making the decision to keep property in the divorce must be looked at in the context of how the asset affects support obligations and the cash flow available to meet them. Conversely, the non-breadwinner and typically the stay-at-home spouse, faces a tough choice on whether or not to keep the family residence because it is often questionable if this is a good financial decision for the non-breadwinner. Keeping the real estate requires paying current obligations (mortgage, taxes, insurance, monthly maintenance), future repairs and, any future ***capital gains tax*** and the ***costs of sale.*** Capital gain taxes and the costs of sale are not owed until the sale of the home, but these items are often very expensive consequences of the decision to keep real estate in the divorce. Therefore, keeping any real estate including the family residence as part of a divorce settlement is a business decision, not an emotional one. This chapter focuses on the issues surrounding the family residence, as opposed to investment real estate, because typically people own family residences but not necessarily investment real estate.

In and Out Spouse

As the result of the property division, if the house is not sold, then one spouse keeps the house. The spouse keeping the family residence is often referred to as the "***in spouse***". The spouse who is bought out (i.e., paid for one-half of the ***net equity***) is often referred to as the "***out spouse***". After the divorce is finalized, and the finances relating to the division of the house has been finalized, it is not uncommon for the "out spouse" to be removed from the deed, yet remain liable for the mortgage obligation on the house. The reason for this is because the only way for the "out spouse" to be removed from a mortgage obligation is for the "in spouse" to refinance the mortgage into his or her name alone. If the "in spouse" is the non-breadwinner, a refinance can prove to be difficult due to the "in spouse's" lack of income, especially in a difficult economic climate. The questions that then arise are (1) Can an equal division of property occur when the "out spouse" remains liable for the mortgage? (2)

Will the "out spouse's" credit be affected? (3) Do the risks outweigh the benefits of the "in spouse" keeping the residence?

Equal Division?

As part of the property division, the "out spouse" should argue that being left potentially liable for the mortgage without ownership in the house is not an equal division of the residence. If the judge agrees, then the "out spouse" may be successful in getting an order for the house to be refinanced or sold, either of which will remove the "out spouse" from the mortgage. Being removed from the mortgage obligation will also improves the ability of the "out spouse" to purchase a home in the future, because a lender is otherwise unlikely to make, in essence, a second mortgage loan to the "out spouse." The "out spouse" should request a "refinance or sale" order even if the case is settled without the help of a judge.

The "in spouse", on the other hand, may resist a sale or refinance, by arguing that the legal requirement for an equal division has been met because the "in spouse" has assumed the responsibility for the mortgage in the property settlement (or court ordered division of assets and liabilities). The logic of this argument is that there is no need to be concerned about the "out spouse's" credit score, potential financial liability or potential future inability to purchase a home, so long as the "in spouse" maintains the payments as required by the bank or lender.

Credit Score Impact

The credit score of the "out spouse" can usually be protected from destruction if the "in spouse" defaults on the mortgage. This can be accomplished by a "fire sale" in the event the "in spouse" defaults on the mortgage. An example of this is that if the "in spouse" is delinquent in payments (i.e., two consecutive payments), then the residence shall be sold at the very best price which will cause an immediate sale (i.e., a "fire sale"). The "out spouse" should insist on receiving any notices of default directly from the "in spouse" as well as from the bank or lender. The greater problem is the "out spouse's" emotional worry that the "in spouse" might default and/or that the credit liability of the old mortgage will likely prevent getting a loan for a new home. There is no solution to this emotional reality.

Risks vs. Benefits

The financial risks of keeping the family residence are relatively quantifiable. The "in spouse" needs to be sure he or she can afford not only the current expenses associated with the residence, but also the future expenses such as repairs, adjustments to the mortgage payment and any future capital gains tax and the costs of sale if the residence is later sold. While the expense figures are quantifiable, the unknown is the "in spouse's" future income of the "in spouse" is the non-breadwinner. In grey divorce, as discussed above, aging affects income such as one's ability to be competitive in the work force and health issues which will likely arise and could impact the ability to maintain the residence. The expense consideration must be balanced against the tax benefits of owning the residence; the cost to replace housing if the residence is sold; the lost opportunity to invest the funds which would result from the sale of the residence which could be used to create a stream of income (i.e., dividend and interest income); and the emotional desire to remain in the residence. These risks and benefits must be weighted with the assistance of a divorce attorney and a financial advisor or accountant.

6

Insurance: Who Is Covered?

Insurance–An ingenious modern game of chance in which the player is permitted to enjoy the comfortable conviction that he is beating the man who keeps the table.

–Ambrose Bierce
The Devil's Dictionary

Health Issues

Health care and health insurance are among the most troublesome issues in grey divorce. Two of the biggest concerns for most people over the age of 50 are the cost of insurance and the ability to obtain or maintain insurance. These issues are no less important when facing a divorce. What people often do not realize is that when they get a divorce, they can no longer be dependent on their former spouse's health insurance policy. There is great uncertainty in the law as our government works to address the cost and ability to obtain health insurance, so working with an experienced and qualified insurance professional is critical.

Coverage Concerns

The reason for this end to dependence is that once the divorce is finalized a former spouse is no longer legally a dependent and therefore cannot legally remain on their spouse's policy. As a result, the cost of obtaining new insurance must be considered in determining spousal support–and this impacts both parties. While the cost is often a manageable problem, the larger problem is if the spouse who is going to lose their health insurance cannot obtain new insurance due to a pre-existing health condition. This is devastating. The problem is worsened when an unemployed breadwinner cannot afford to contribute toward the non-breadwinner's health insurance cost.

If a spouse cannot obtain new insurance as an individual (as opposed to a group policy), then alternative solutions must be explored, such as agreeing to a ***legal separation*** instead of a divorce thereby maintaining the status of being married; obtaining employment where a group plan is offered; or COBRA and other subsidized options. The best way to handle this very expensive and difficult problem is for the parties to cooperate in the solution. An uncovered medical expense is not in anyone's best interest.

Breadwinner Health Care Costs

Another difficult economic reality is that often in grey divorce, one or both parties have increased health care and insurance expenses. These expenses are mostly met from the breadwinner's income. Exploring ways to mitigate these expenses is critical. Options to examine include one or both spouse obtaining long-term care insurance, group health insurance, government-aided health insurance, disability insurance, and Social Security benefits. Liquidation of assets (for example, selling real property or accessing retirement plans), and reduced living expenses may be required to meet the ongoing expenses for one or both spouses.

Non-Breadwinner Health Care Costs

If the breadwinner becomes unemployed, he or she may not be able to afford to contribute toward the health care and insurance expense of the non-breadwinner. Exploring ways to mitigate these expenses is critical. Options to examine are the same as those for the breadwinner: long-term care insurance, group health insurance (see below), government-aided health insurance, disability insurance, Social Security benefits, liquidation of assets (for example, selling real property or accessing retirement plans), and reduced living expenses. In order to obtain group health insurance, if the non-breadwinner has been unemployed, the non-breadwinner must re-enter the workforce and get a job that provides group health insurance. The expense (if any) is typically quite low and there is no medical qualification for the insurance. This is often the most important reason for the non-breadwinner to re-enter the workforce later in life.

7

Taxes:
Who Pays and Why?

Should five percent appear too small
Be thankful I don't take it all
'Cause I'm the taxman
Yeah I'm the taxman

–The Beatles

It's not easy to find a benefit in divorce, but there are tax advantages which are positive, sometimes only for one spouse, but often for both spouses. There may be other tax benefits or consequences other than those identified below, but these are some of the basics. With that being said both spouses should consult with their own individual accountant to determine the tax consequences associated with their individual situation. The IRS rules for claiming theses tax filing statuses are complex and they are especially complicated in the year the spouses separate.

Child Support

A spouse receiving child support does not have to pay taxes on this money. It is tax free. This means, the spouse paying child support cannot deduct this payment. While there is no tax consequence associated with the payment or receipt of child support, there are benefits to certain tax status associated with children, two of which are important in determining the amount of support to be paid: Head of Household status and the Dependency Exemption.

Head of Household You qualify for Head of Household status, if all of the following requirements are met:

- You are unmarried or "considered unmarried" on the last day of the year.
- You paid more than half the cost of keeping up a home for the year.
- A "qualifying person" lived with you in the home for more than half the year (except for temporary absences, such as school).

Considered Unmarried You are considered unmarried on the last day of the tax year if you meet all the following tests.

- You file a separate return. A separate return includes a return claiming married filing separately, single, or head of household filing status.
- You paid more than half the cost of keeping up your home for the tax year.
- Your spouse did not live in your home during the last six months of the tax year. Your spouse is considered

to live in your home even if he or she is temporarily absent due to special circumstances.

- Your home was the main home of your child, stepchild, or foster child for more than half the year.

- You must be able to claim an exemption for the child. This can occur because you are the ***custodial parent***; or, if the custodial parent releases the exemption to the ***non-custodial parent***.

If parties share custody equally (i.e., 50/50), each party may each be able to qualify for Head of Household status. If there is only one child, the parties can alternate the years that they each claim Head of Household status and insure their custody agreement sets forth the requirements to achieve this status. If there are two or more children, the tax benefits for the children can be divided between the parents to insure they each qualify each year for Head of Household status and can adjust the dependency exemptions to minimize taxes.

The Dependency Exemption will, by default, belong to the spouse who qualifies for Head of Household status (i.e., custodial parent). If a spouse does not qualify for Head of Household status, they can still benefit from the Dependency Exemption if the custodial parent agrees to release (i.e., waive) the exemption to the non-Head of Household spouse using the specially designated IRS form. This is done to minimize a parent's overall taxes thereby increasing the net income into his or her household. However, it is important to know that the Dependency Exemption phases out, and is therefore of no the spouse who earns in excess of the IRS limits for this benefit. Parties who cooperate can find a way to financially benefit from these rules.

Spousal Support

A spouse receiving spousal support pursuant to a written agreement or court order must pay taxes on this money; the spouse paying spousal support receives a tax deduction (unlike in child support). It is critical that spousal support be in a written agreement stating that it shall last no longer than the death of the recipient spouse (although it can end on an earlier designated date, such as remarriage or a date certain). It is important for the tax consequences of spousal support to be taken into consideration in the settlement of the entire case.

If agreed between the spouses, the settlement agreement can structure the spousal support as a non-taxable payment thereby allowing for more flexible tax planning. If parties litigate their matter and allow a judge to decide the issue, the spousal support paid will be taxable to the recipient and deductible by the payor. In that case, there is no option for a non-taxable designation.

Understanding these tax rules is particularly important in grey divorce because, due to the tax deduction of the spousal support payment, the breadwinner can reduce taxes and increase cash flow at year-end thereby allowing for year-end retirement planning. If the spousal support deduction is not important for the breadwinner, negotiating a non-taxable spousal support arrangement means paying a lower amount of spousal support because the non-breadwinner will not need to pay taxes on her spousal support, thereby freeing money for retirement funding or living expenses on a monthly basis.

Property Division

Property transferred between spouses in connection with their divorce is a tax-free event. However, it is important to know the *tax basis* and hidden future taxes associated with an asset which is awarded to each party in the divorce. For example:

- Special attention needs to be paid to the capital gains tax exclusion rules associated with the family residence when it is sold.
- You need to know the rules concerning keeping your lower property tax basis when you sell a home and buy a new one after age 55.
- If you keep the investment real estate in the divorce, you need to be aware of the capital gain taxes associated with the real estate when sold.

- Some retirement accounts will distribute payments upon retirement as tax-free payments; others will require the payment of taxes. This needs to be understood not only from a future cash flow perspective, but also in terms of the valuation of assets in the divorce. A retirement plan which is subject to taxes is not worth the same value as cash in the bank. The true value (after taxes) should be considered in the property division.

The tax issues in grey divorce can be significant because many people at this stage in life have held assets for many years which means, many of these assets carry tax consequences which will come to light years after the divorce.

Attorneys' Fees

Generally, fees charged by attorneys, accountants, appraisers and other experts in connection with the divorce, child custody and similar family law disputes are not deductible by either party because they are considered personal expenses. However, if these expenses are incurred to obtain taxable income, such as establishing or changing taxable spousal support, then the legal fees are tax deductible. Because one of the biggest issues in grey divorce is spousal support, a large component of the attorneys' fees will be tax deductible. It is critical that your attorney provide detailed billing statements so your accountant can determine what portion of the fees are tax deductible.

Innocent Spouse Relief

Beyond the tax implications of the divorce settlement, the issue of tax returns filed prior to the divorce frequently arises. Often this is because, in couples over the age of 50, their more traditional financial attitudes have meant that the husband has been responsible throughout the marriage for preparing or otherwise overseeing the annual tax filing. The wife, particularly if she is a non-breadwinner often simply signs the tax forms because she trusts her husband or is less informed about the family's finances. Regardless, if the spouses signed a joint tax return when married, they agreed to be jointly and individually responsible for the tax and any interest or penalty due on the joint tax return, even if they later divorce.

Often in divorce, the tax returns are questioned as to their accuracy, sometimes because the Internal Revenue Service (IRS) initiates collection activity due to an understated or underpaid income tax liability. It is when the collection effort by the IRS commences that a spouse typically starts questioning the content of the tax return and whether relief from liability is possible under the ***innocent spouse*** program. Generally speaking, an innocent spouse is a taxpayer who did not know and did not have reason to know that his or her spouse understated or underpaid an income tax liability.

During a divorce tax returns are also typically analyzed by the lawyers and accountants for both sides often raising concerns about the returns. If taxes are due on any tax return, it is important to review the circumstances surrounding its preparation to determine if there is any benefit in seeking innocent spouse relief.

8

Bankruptcy: What Is the Impact?

Debt is the worst poverty.

−M. G. Lichtwer

Bankruptcy is an increasingly common phenomenon for people over the age of 50. Recent statistics show that during the past decade the average debt for households headed by people 55 or older nearly doubled. As just one consequence, debtors age 55 to 64 accounted for nearly 20% of bankruptcy filers in 2009, an increase of one-fifth in just two years. Older Americans are suffering from debt because of a variety of problems–from unexpected job losses late in life and underemployment to overwhelming medical bills and providing financial help to their children and grandchildren, analysts say. Making the issue even more serious is that they have little time to climb out of debt. All these issues combine to make bankruptcy a more common occurrence in grey divorces, and that can add substantial financial complications.[5]

---

5 "For Many Over 55, Debt Defers Dreams," USA Today, 10/25/10, reprinted in http://www.aarp.org/money/credit-loans-debt/news-10-2010/for_many_over_55_debt_defers_dreams.html

Bankruptcy Stay

Very specific and important implications occur when bankruptcy and divorce occur at the same time. If a bankruptcy is filed by either spouse while a divorce action is pending, the divorce is "stayed" (i.e., placed on hold). The only way for the divorce to proceed is for either the bankruptcy case to be concluded; or, if a "relief from stay" (i.e., no longer on hold) is obtained from the bankruptcy court authorizing the divorce proceeding to continue while the bankruptcy is pending. Serious financial sanctions to the parties, lawyers and state court judges (i.e., the judge in the divorce action) can be imposed by the federal bankruptcy judge if the rules are not followed. Therefore, if a bankruptcy is commenced or is contemplated at the same time a divorce action is pending, it is critical that bankruptcy and divorce counsel are consulted.

Non-Dischargeable Debts

A common misconception about bankruptcy is that it can be used to *discharge* all debts and obligations, including child support, spousal support, and past due support (also known as "support arrearages"). That is not the case. Child support and spousal support orders are referred to by federal law as "domestic support obligations" and are considered "non-dischargeable debts." Any support obligation incurred before, during or after the date a bankruptcy is sought, cannot be discharged. This includes interest that accrues on those debts. Thus, a payor of child support or spousal support who files for bankruptcy must continue to meet his/her support obligations.

Just as support is non-dischargeable, so is the *equalization payment*–that payment from one spouse to another to create an equal division of assets in the divorce. Prior to a change in law, it used to be that parties could negotiate the division of assets in a way that one would knowingly assume assets in the divorce which might be excluded by law from the bankruptcy (such as retirement accounts) in exchange for paying the other spouse money to equalize the assets. Then, the spouse owing the money to his or her former spouse would file bankruptcy to discharge the obligation. Under the old laws, this allowed the spouse to keep their retirement accounts obtained in the divorce and discharge the amount they were supposed to pay the other spouse. This clearly deprived one spouses of his/her share of the community property.

Because this was patently unfair, the law changed. Now, it is not possible to, in essence, walk out of divorce court with an obligation owed to a former spouse and then walk across the street to bankruptcy court to be rid of that same obligation. Except in extreme cases, bankruptcy court will not serve as a safe haven for unloading obligations owed to one's spouse as a result of the property division and is never a place to unload child and spousal support obligations.

With that being said, it does not mean that bankruptcy is an inappropriate option when credit card, medical bills and other dischargeable obligations mount. Bankruptcy no doubt at the least harms, if not destroys, one's credit. However, for individuals over 50, credit rating may not be critical. Credit is only important if you need to obtain credit for loans (mortgages, credit cards, unsecured lines of credit, etc). If a home is already owned, an apartment secured, cars owned and financial resources exist to assist in living expenses, then the credit score may not be as important to having a clean financial slate.

The pros and cons of bankruptcy, along with the timing of the bankruptcy must be discussed with a bankruptcy attorney, a financial advisor and a divorce attorney.

9

Estate Planning: Are Your Wishes Honored?

Despite his immense gusto for life, in a rather jovial cozy way Churchill never minded contemplating the mystery of death. Once a friend inquired: "What makes you think you will reach the bar of Heaven?" He interjected with solemn assurance: "Surely the Almighty must observe the principles of English common law and consider a man innocent until proven guilty."

–Winston S. Churchill, *New York Times*, 2-1-65; 22C; col. 6.

Grey Divorce Considerations

Most divorce lawyers are not estate planners yet estate planning is vitally important as part of the divorce process and after the divorce. For parties in grey divorce, estate planning considerations are more important than for younger individuals because of the age and health of those involved. This is true whether or not the divorcing spouses already have a trust or will. Many people believe that death is an unlikely possibility anytime soon if they are healthy. This may be statistically true, but accidents and unfortunate events do occur, making estate planning a major consideration during and after a grey divorce.

In 1967, psychiatrists, Thomas Holmes and Richard Rahe examined the medical records of over 5,000 medical patients as a way to determine whether stressful events might cause illnesses. Their results were published as the Social Readjustment Rating Scale (SRRS), known more commonly as the Holmes and Rahe Stress Scale. Results showed that the stress of a divorce is considered the second most stressful event of a person's life which can contribute to illness; the first being the death of a spouse. This means in grey divorce this reality can cause the onset of illness and sometimes death.

This reality means that without planning, the person you are divorcing, or just divorced, may end up making decisions about your money and healthcare if you are incapacitated; and, receiving your share of the community property or a portion of your *separate property*, when you die. If this is not your desire, consider the following carefully.

Real Property

Many married people hold title to real property that lists their spouse as ***joint tenant with rights of survivorship***. This means that when one spouse dies, the other spouse receives the entire property. As just discussed, you may not want your spouse to receive your one-half interest in the property if you die during the divorce, but would instead prefer for your share to go to your children, parent, sibling, or charity.

In California, without the consent of your spouse, but upon giving notice, title can be changed so that your current wishes will prevail in the unfortunate event of your death during or after the divorce. By doing this, each person is allowed to provide in a will who will receive his or her one-half interest in the property if they die. It is important to understand that it is not sufficient to just change title; a will must also be prepared stating what will happen to your interest in the house or other real property upon your death.

Trusts & Wills

If there is a ***trust*** or a ***will*** at the time a divorce is expected, it is important to consider revoking the trust and will in conjunction with a general review of the estate plan. If these documents do not represent your current wishes, then they need to be changed. California law provides that, once a marriage is ***dissolved***, the ***dissolution*** revokes any transfers of property to the former spouse provided for in the will; however, if a spouse dies during the divorce process, his or her estate will be distributed as set forth in those documents. This could mean that the same person who is fighting to keep certain assets from you in the divorce may in fact receive those very assets in the event of your death. To avoid this situation it is necessary to change the documentation to ensure that your separate property and your one-half of the community property are passed to another person of your choosing.

Trust Funding

After any divorce action is filed in the State of California, ***Standard Family Law Restraining Orders*** are automatically issued. One of the restraining orders prevents funding a trust during a divorce. Upon notice to the other party, the restraining orders allow you to revoke an existing trust and you can even create a new trust; however, you cannot actually fund the new trust. Therefore, you thus need a will if you die during the divorce. Although dying with a will and an unfunded trust will mean your estate will go through ***probate***, this is a better result than dying with a formerly created trust which does not now reflect your wishes. The new will allows you to provide for the distribution of your separate property and your one-half of the community property should you die before the divorce is complete. Upon the conclusion of the divorce action, the restraining orders no longer apply and a trust can be funded with the property (community and separate) awarded to you in the divorce judgment.

Beneficiary Designations

Separate from preparing a trust or a will is the question of ***beneficiary*** designations on bank accounts, retirement accounts and life insurance policies. Once a divorce action is filed there is no question that, in accordance with the Standard Family Law Restraining Orders, these beneficiary designations cannot be changed during the divorce proceeding. Whether or not these beneficiary designations can be changed before actually filing a divorce action is an open question in the law. Many lawyers (and probably judges) believe that changing the beneficiary designations near the start of a divorce may be a breach of a duty (i.e., responsibility) that spouses owe to each other because one spouse is unilaterally changing the status quo. Breaching a duty can be financially devastating in California because the law provides, in essence, for a type of monetary damage to be paid by the spouse who breached the duty to the other spouse when this occurs. Therefore, it is best to discuss this issue with a family law attorney before changing the beneficiary designations.

Durable Powers of Attorney

A ***durable power of attorney*** allows you to nominate a person to act on your behalf (your "agent") with regards to finances in the event of your ***incapacity***. As with many estate planning and other documents created during a marriage, it is not uncommon for spouses to name each other as the person to make financial decisions for each other. However, when divorce is near, it is highly unlikely that you still want your spouse to act in that capacity on your behalf. Such powers allow your agent to have broad or narrowly defined powers as you wish, but can include some or all of the following:

- Use your assets to pay your everyday expenses and those of your family.
- Buy, sell, maintain, pay taxes on, and mortgage real estate and other property.
- Collect Social Security, Medicare, or other government benefits.
- Invest your money in stocks, bonds, and mutual funds.
- Handle transactions with banks and other financial institutions.
- Buy and sell insurance policies and annuities for you.
- File and pay your taxes.
- Operate your small business.
- Claim property you inherit or are otherwise entitled to.
- Transfer property to a trust you've already created.
- Tire someone to represent you in court.
- Manage your retirement accounts.

For most people going through a divorce, trust is often missing in the relationship. The durable power of attorney is premised upon trusting the agent who will act on your behalf. Therefore, revoking an existing durable power of attorney and executing a new one is critical when divorce is near.

Advance Health Care Directives

Most people, if they have done estate planning, have directives in place which set forth their wishes concerning their health care in the event of incapacity and certain directives upon death. Typically, married people name their spouses as the person in charge of their welfare in the event of such an unfortunate event.

If at any time you named your spouse as the person who has decision-making power over your health care or other similar decisions, you may want to reconsider this designation when divorce is near. If you have not documented these rights, then you may want to do so and designate a person of your choosing. Otherwise, your spouse will be legally the person allowed to make these decisions on your behalf, which is not what most people want in the midst of a divorce. Once the divorce is final, the law essentially revokes the ***Advance Health Care Directive*** naming a former spouse, but does not revoke the authority of anyone else, such as a former in-law. Therefore, it is critical the Advance Health Care Directive is reviewed immediately upon divorce, if not sooner.

Your Choices

- You have the right to give instructions about your own health care.
- You also have the right to name someone else to make health care decisions for you.
- You have the right to write down your wishes about donation of organs and the selection of your primary physician.

Advance Health Care Directive–Lets You:

- Name another person as agent to make health care decisions for you if you are unable to make your own decisions. You can also have your agent make decisions for you right away, even if you are still able to make your own decisions.

- Also name an alternate agent to act for you if your first choice is not willing, able or reasonably available to make decisions for you.

- You can nominate a person to make long term care decisions for you such as long term placement care options, where you will live, etc. This requires the nomination of a conservator.

- Your agent *may not be*:

    - an operator or employee of a community care facility or a residential care facility where you are receiving care.

    - your supervising health care provider (the doctor managing your care)

- an employee of the health care institution where you are receiving care, unless your agent is related to you or is a coworker.

Your agent may make all health care decisions for you, *unless* you limit the authority of your agent. You do not need to limit the authority of your agent.

If you want to limit the authority of your agent you must indicate the limits of authority of your agent.

If you choose not to limit the authority of your agent, your agent will have the right to:

- Generally, consent or refuse consent to any care, treatment, service, or procedure to maintain, diagnose, or otherwise affect a physical or mental condition.
- Choose or discharge health care providers (i.e. choose a doctor for you) and institutions.
- Agree or disagree to diagnostic tests, surgical procedures, and medication plans.

- Agree or disagree with providing, withholding, or withdrawal of artificial feeding and fluids and all other forms of health care, including cardiopulmonary resuscitation (CPR).
- After your death make anatomical gifts (donate organs/tissues), authorize an autopsy, and make decisions about what will be done with your body.

Donation of Organs You can write down your wishes about donating your bodily organs and tissues following your death.

Primary Physician You can select a physician to have primary or main responsibility for your health care.

Estate Planning After Divorce

Estate planning is critical before and during divorce. It is also critical after divorce not only to ensure your wishes are accurately stated in the event of your death, or your incapacity, but also to make sure your estate plan and your ***divorce judgment*** do not conflict with each other.

Often as part of a divorce judgment, one of the parties is required to maintain life insurance for the other party or for the benefit of children; or, the parties have agreed to a certain disposition of property upon their deaths; or are required to maintain certain beneficiary designations. If you are under any of these directives after the divorce, it is critical that your estate planning attorney review your estate plan to make sure you are in compliance with the divorce judgment.

10

Professional Advice: Who Can You Talk To?

Knowledge is of two kinds. We know a subject ourselves, or we know where we can find information upon it.

–Samuel Johnson
in James Boswell, *Life of Johnson* (April 18, 1775); Act. 66)

In addition to the legal issues which are presented in a grey divorce, it is important for divorcing spouses in this age group to reach out to other professional advisors to ensure their financial future and increasing health issues are addressed. In the grey divorce, due to increasing age, often declining health, loss of income due to retirement or disability and statistically the greater chance of death, the issues are especially immediate. Therefore, engaging a good team of professionals as soon as possible is critical. While the following professionals should be consulted in any divorce, regardless of age, the issues are more acute in the grey divorce.

Estate Planner

Everyone's estate plan should be reviewed periodically, but especially during and after a divorce. It is important for two reasons: first, to ensure that property will be transferred to the desired person, charity or institution upon death; second, to review tax planning in light of one's age, health and wealth after divorce. A very important consideration during a divorce is to review and update Advance Heath

Care Directives and Powers of Attorney. Because spouses in a grey divorce often have failing health, it is important that a trusted person will make critical decisions in the event of hospitalization or incapacity of either divorced spouse.

Insurance Agent

A dependent spouse on a health insurance policy will lose his or her health insurance upon divorce. For the spouse who will be removed from the insurance policy, it may be difficult and potentially impossible to obtain health insurance due to age, health and pre-existing conditions. Therefore, long-term care insurance must be considered as a possible alternative to make sure that some benefits toward in-home or residential care can be accessed. Long-term care insurance should also be considered even when health insurance is available because it is a different benefit than health insurance and is typically a small expense as compared to the cost of home or residential care later in life.

Financial Advisor

For many people over the age of 50, retirement planning is in process and maybe even right on target until the time a divorce occurs. The money saved by the couple is now going to have to support two separate households, often as income is decreasing. It is critical to consult with a financial advisor to re-evaluate the retirement financial plan for each person individually in light of the division of assets and the payment or receipt of spousal support.

Accountant

An accountant's advice likely will impact the estate plan, insurance decisions and the financial plan. It should be part of the decision-making process throughout the divorce and after the divorce. The accountant can assess the division of assets negotiated in the divorce to maximize tax benefits, explain fully the tax effect of any potential settlement, and advise how estate taxes will impact each party's financial situations upon death after the divorce.

Family Law Attorneys and Mediators

Throughout this book it has been emphasized that grey divorce involves complex financial issues and difficult financial choices. It may be tempting for the two parties in grey divorce, either of whom may be experiencing difficult financial circumstances or may fear such circumstances in the future, to proceed without legal representation. However, to make such a choice means struggling with the complexities of the laws and the legal system and likely will produce an undesirable outcome.

Going through a divorce takes a big emotional toll, but proceeding with a divorce without any legal guidance may lead to adverse consequences which possibly may not or cannot be reversed. To be the most economical about spending attorneys' fees, both parties must work very hard to put aside their emotions and work together, with the assistance of a mediator or with cooperative attorneys, to help them to resolve their financial and custodial issues in an economical and legally proper way. Yes, this costs some money, but the cost is no doubt a fraction of the money that is spent in an adversarial situation.

Grey divorce requires cooperation in a spirit of partnership that once made the marriage viable. Working cooperatively is the best way to maximize outcomes and minimize the negatives, so that each of the parties to the grey divorce can move past the pain and get on with their lives for a better future.

11

Final Thoughts

I started practicing family law when I graduated from law school in 1994. While I was quite certain I was going to enjoy practicing law, never did I expect to be passionate about practicing law. Family law made me passionate because I have the opportunity each and every day to make a difference in individuals' lives. At first blush many people, lawyers and non-lawyers, think handling a divorce is simple. The fact is family law is one of the most complex areas of the law. This is because family law attorneys must have a broad knowledge about a lot of issues including but certainly not limited to: children, money, property, finance, accounting, business, human nature, litigation, mediation, negotiation, taxes, insurance, estate planning, bankruptcy, and much more.

After practicing for more than 17 years, what I am certain about is that what sets a family law attorney apart is not just intelligence, but also intuition. I grew up in a family of entrepreneurs. I have always considered myself to be one of the intuitive lawyers and this book is an example of my intuition. While many lawyers are seeking to represent celebrities and "high net worth" individuals, I do not hear family law attorneys discussing or recognizing that our population is aging, that divorce among our aging population is increasing, and that brings unique issues in a divorce–in grey divorce. It is my intuition which tells me this topic is not at the forefront of the legal community yet grey divorce–divorce which occurs after the age of 50–brings about unique issues.

I have always viewed the attorney-client relationship to be a partnership and the more knowledge my client has about an issue involved in their legal matter, the better the partnership. While divorce is prevalent especially among our greying population, the conversation concerning this subject is not. My intuition, and now hopefully your intuition, focuses on important topics in these cases, making you–the client–better informed and better able to participate as a partner with your lawyer to achieve the best outcome possible when the unfortunate event of divorce occurs.

12
Glossary

Advance health care directive Any adult with capacity may give an individual health care instruction orally or in writing, and the instruction may be limited to take effect on the occurrence of a specified condition.

Annulment A legal proceeding seeking to nullify the marriage for reasons existing at the time of the marriage, such that no valid marriage ever occurred. A marriage may be invalid from its inception because of irregularities in statutory formalization procedures (ordinarily, license, solemnization and authentication) or because of other legal impediments that, notwithstanding proper formalization, render the marriage void or voidable (incestuous, bigamous, induced by fraud or force, party under age of consent, etc.)

Beneficiary One who benefits from a transfer of property or other arrangement such as proceeds on death of an insured; a person named in a will or a trust to receive specified property upon the death of the person who created the will or trust.

Breadwinner One whose earnings are the primary source of support for one's dependents.

Capital gains tax The profit realized on the sale or exchange of a capital asset. The gain is the difference between the cost or the adjusted basis of an asset and the net proceeds from the sale or exchange of such asset. The actual calculation of the tax must be done by an accountant.

Child support Money paid by one parent to another toward the expenses of the children of the relationship.

Community property Property owned in common by husband and wife each having an undivided one-half interest by reason of their marital status. Under a community property system, one-half of the earnings of each spouse is considered to be owned by the other spouse. There are nine states with community property systems: Louisiana, Texas, New Mexico, Arizona, California, Washington, Idaho, Nevada and Wisconsin.

Costs of sale The costs associated with the sale of real property such as the costs for escrow, real estate commissions, appraisals, and title.

Custodial parent The parent who, at any given time, is responsible for the care and control of child. Also refers to the parent who has custodial time with the child more than the other parent.

Date marital status is terminated The date the court declares the legal status of being married is ended and the individuals are returned to single status.

Derivative Social Security benefits (also derivative benefits) A former spouse married for 10 years or longer to a spouse who paid into the Social Security system may be entitled to receive a separate benefit based upon the worker spouse's contributions into the Social Security system

Discharge The release of a debtor from all of his or her debts which are provable in bankruptcy, except those which are excepted by the Bankruptcy Code.

Dissolution The act of terminating a marriage; divorce.

Dissolved To terminate. See ***Dissolution***

Divorce judgment The official document which sets forth the rights, claims and responsibilities of the parties to the action and that which contains the date the marital status is terminated. See ***Date marital status is terminated***

Durable power of attorney An instrument in writing whereby one person (a principal) appoints another person and his or her agent and gives that person authority to perform certain specified acts on behalf of the principal. The durable power of attorney becomes or remains effective in the event the person (principal) should later become disabled.

Earning capacity In a family law matter, for purposes of determining support, it is not the amount a person can theoretically earn but is the amount which an individual could realistically earn under circumstances including health, age, mental and physical conditions and training and given an actual opportunity to earn that amount.

Equalization payment A payment from one spouse to another to make the division of community property equal.

Grey divorce The demographic trend of an increasing divorce rate for older ("grey-haired") couples in what had been long-lasting marriages; also marriages that end when one or both spouses are over the age of 50.

Incapacity (also incapacitated) A person who is impaired by mental illness or deficiency, physical illness or disability, advanced age or other causes which results in the lack of sufficient understanding to make or communicate responsible decisions concerning his or her person.

Innocent spouse (also innocent spouse relief) A taxpayer who did not know and did not have reason to know that his or her spouse understated or underpaid an income tax liability.

In spouse The spouse who remains living in the family residence during the divorce process.

Joint tenants with right of survivorship Type of ownership of real or personal property by two or more persons who own an undivided interest in the whole property. Up to the death of one joint tenant, the remaining joint tenants automatically become the owner of the interest of the deceased joint tenant.

Legal separation A court order setting forth custody, support and property under which a married couple remain legally married but will live separately.

Long-term marriage A marriage of at least 10 years in length between the date of marriage and the date spouses separate.

Marital standard of living The standard of living established during the marriage.

Net equity The fair market value minus the debt on real property.

Non-breadwinner The spouse with no earnings or less earnings than the breadwinner.

Non-custodial parent The parent who, at any given time, does not have the responsibility for the care and control of child. Also refers to the parent who has custodial time with the child less than the other parent.

Out spouse The spouse who moves out of the family residence during the divorce process.

Probate Court procedure by which a will is proved to be valid or invalid. May include the administration of an estate after a person's death which involves collecting the deceased person's assets, liquidating liabilities, paying necessary taxes, and distributing property to heirs.

Separate property Property which belongs entirely to one spouse. In a community property state, it is property acquired before marriage or acquired after marriage by gift or inheritance together with the rents, issues and profits therefrom.

Short-term marriage A marriage lasting less than 10 years in length between the date of marriage and the date spouses separate.

Social Security benefits When earnings stop or are reduced because the worker retires, dies, or becomes disabled, monthly cash benefits are paid by the federal government to replace part of the earnings the person or family has lost.

Spousal support Money paid from one spouse to another for his or her maintenance.

Standard Family Law Restraining Orders In California, court orders automatically issued when a dissolution (divorce) is commenced which, with limited exceptions, prohibit the transfer of property, incurring debts, changing beneficiaries or removing a child from the state without the consent of the other party or permission from the court. These orders are effective until the divorce is final.

Tax basis The cost of property acquired, increased for any capital improvements and decreased by the amount of depreciation allowed or allowable.

Trust A legal entity created by a person (grantor) for the benefit of others (beneficiaries).

Will A document which sets forth a person's wishes about how his or her property will be transferred after his or her death.

About Marlo Van Oorschot, author of "How To Survive Grey Divorce"

Marlo Van Oorschot has gained a reputation during more than 17 years as a respected Los Angeles-based family law attorney who has helped hundreds of clients resolve divorce, child custody, child and spousal support and property disputes. She is the founding and managing partner of Law Offices of Marlo Van Oorschot, APLC.

Ms. Van Oorschot focuses her advice and guidance on helping people take the steps necessary to emerge into the next phase of their lives empowered with knowledge, a new perspective and productive solutions. She excels at using the right process at the right time for each individual client, which includes where appropriate, litigation, mediation and collaborative proceedings as the latter of which are alternatives to courtroom controversy. Her practical approach is central to *How To Survive Grey Divorce: What You Need to Know About Divorce After 50*. As she explains, "A great way to help alleviate your concerns about divorce is to learn more about the process. Reviewing this information can help you understand what you face in grey divorce, and enable you to frame questions and develop answers and strategy you hadn't thought of before."

Ms. Van Oorschot's years of experience have taught her that the best approach to a divorce is reflected in a specific process, the phrase which she has trademarked as "Strategy. Guidance. Teamwork.™" These words describe the way in which Ms. Van Oorschot assesses the needs of each specific client and works with the client as a trusted partner at every step in the divorce proceeding.

Ms. Van Oorschot limits her practice to family law matters, has been named as a "Rising Star Super Lawyer" and "Super Lawyer" by Los Angeles Magazine, and holds the highest "AV® Preeminent™ Peer Rating" from the authoritative Martindale-Hubbell guide.

In writing Surviving Grey Divorce, Ms. Van Oorschot continues a tradition of education and outreach that is fundamental to her legal career. She regularly blogs on family law issues at www.mvolaw.com. Her more detailed discussions of divorce-related concerns have appeared in such authoritative publications as the Los Angeles Daily Law Journal ("Your Parents' Grey Divorce: No More Ozzie and Harriet," an earlier and much shorter version of this book published July 25, 2011) and the American Bar

Association's GPSolo magazine ("Planning for Your Divorce … and Your Next Marriage," October/November 2008). Ms. Van Oorschot has been quoted in media outlets (for example, an Internet radio interview on prenuptial agreements found on her website at www.mvolaw.com) and has been a featured speaker in professional education programs like the West LegalEd Center audio podcast, "The Grey Divorce: Its Impact on the Lawyer, the Lawyer's Practice and the Lawyer's Second Season" (September 20, 2011).

Ms. Van Oorschot is married and lives in Los Angeles with her husband.

Ms. Van Oorschot can be contacted at:

Law Offices of Marlo Van Oorschot, APLC
10513 Santa Monica Boulevard
Los Angeles, CA 90025
Phone: (310) 820-3414
Email: mvo@mvolaw.com

www.ingramcontent.com/pod-product-compliance
Lightning Source LLC
Chambersburg PA
CBHW070203100426
42743CB00013B/3026